SUKUMA

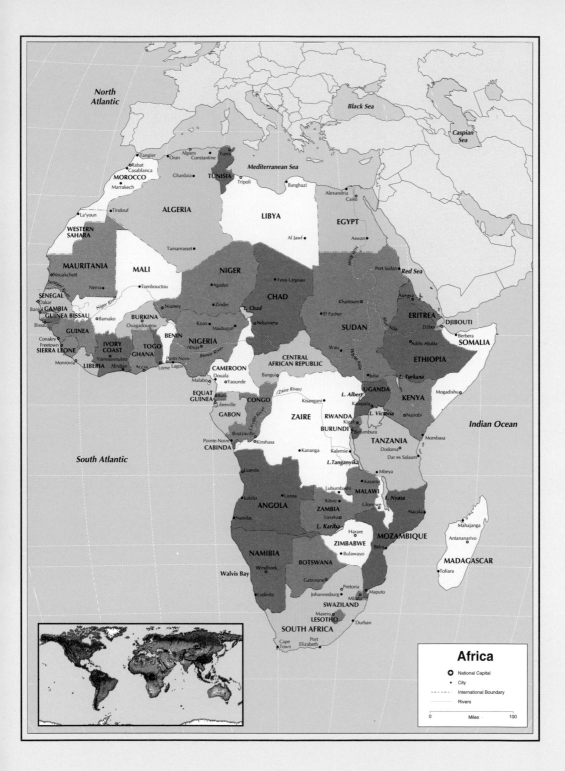

The Heritage Library of African Peoples

SUKUMA

Aimée Bessire and Mark Bessire

THE ROSEN PUBLISHING GROUP, INC.
NEW YORK

Dedication:
For our Sukuma and American families who now know one another.

Published in 1997 by The Rosen Publishing Group, Inc.
29 East 21st Street, New York, NY 10010

First Edition

Manufactured in the United States of America

Library of Congress Cataloging-in-Publication Data

Bessire, Aimée.
    Sukuma / Aimée Bessire and Mark Bessire. — 1st ed.
      p.   cm. — (The heritage library of African peoples)
    Includes bibliographical references and index.
    Summary: Surveys the history, culture, and contemporary life of the Sukuma people of Tanzania.
    ISBN 0-8239-1992-7
    1. Sukuma (African people)—History—Juvenile literature.
2. Sukuma (African people)—Social life and customs—Juvenile literature.   3. Sukumaland (Tanzania)—Social life and customs—Juvenile literature. [1. Sukuma (African people)] I. Bessire, Mark. II. Title. III. Series.
D1443.3.S86B47   1996
306′.089′96394—dc20
                                    96-38236
                                           CIP
                                           AC

Contents

INTRODUCTION

THERE IS EVERY REASON FOR US TO KNOW something about Africa and to understand its past and the way of life of its peoples. Africa is a rich continent that has for centuries provided the world with art, culture, labor, wealth, and natural resources. It has vast mineral deposits, fossil fuels, and commercial crops.

But perhaps most important is the fact that fossil evidence indicates that human beings originated in Africa. The earliest traces of human beings and their tools are almost two million years old. Their descendants have migrated throughout the world. To be human is to be of African descent.

The experiences of the peoples who stayed in Africa are as rich and as diverse as of those who established themselves elsewhere. This series of books describes their environment, their modes of subsistence, their relationships, and their customs and beliefs. The books present the variety of languages, histories, cultures, and religions that are to be found on the African continent. They demonstrate the historical linkages between African peoples and the way contemporary Africa has been affected by European colonial rule.

Africa is large, complex, and diverse. It encompasses an area of more than 11,700,000 square miles. The United States, Europe, and India could fit easily into it. The sheer size is an indication of the continent's great variety in geography, terrain, climate, flora, fauna, peoples, languages, and cultures.

Much of contemporary Africa has been shaped by European colonial rule, industrialization, urbanization, and the demands of a world economic system. For more than seventy years, large regions of Africa were ruled by Great Britain, France, Belgium, Portugal, and Spain. African peoples from various ethnic, linguistic, and cultural backgrounds were brought together to form colonial states.

For decades Africans struggled to gain their independence. It was not until after World War II that the colonial territories became independent African states. Today almost all of Africa is ruled by Africans. Large numbers of Africans live in modern cities. Rural Africa is also being transformed, and yet its people still engage in many of their customs and beliefs.

Contemporary circumstances and natural events have not always been kind to ordinary Africans. Today, however, new popular social movements and technological innovations pose great promise for future development.

George C. Bond, Ph.D., Director
Institute of African Studies
Columbia University, New York

The Sukuma are famous for their dance competitions. The drummer seen here beats out a rhythm while keeping his eyes on the performers.

chapter

1

THE LAND AND THE PEOPLE

THE SUKUMA PEOPLE LIVE IN AN AREA called Usukuma in Tanzania. The Usukuma region is located to the west and south of Lake Victoria, the second largest lake in the world.

▼ *UTAMUDUNI* (TRADITIONAL CULTURE) ▼

The Sukuma culture is the largest in Tanzania. The Sukuma people are now expressing a renewed interest in their traditional culture, called *utamuduni*. They are finding many new ways to celebrate their traditions.

Tradition exists in harmony with contemporary life, rather than in conflict with it. This allows *utamuduni* to thrive alongside modern development and economic growth in Usukuma.

Traditional doctors, chiefs, artists, and dancers are leading figures in the revival of *utamuduni*. They all mix tradition and modern influences in dynamic new ways. While they

Most of Usukuma is rural. However, the city of Mwanza seen here is one of the fastest growing centers in Tanzania.

follow and honor *utamuduni*, they are also sensitive to the many social and political changes occurring in Usukuma.

Mwanza, the largest urban center in Usukuma, is one of the largest and fastest growing cities in Tanzania. While most of Usukuma is rural and many Sukuma live in the countryside, people throughout Tanzania and central Africa are flocking to Mwanza to find work in one of its many growing industries.

Many Sukuma still work as farmers, merchants, builders, and traditional doctors; but, in today's economy, others work in communications, health, shipping, transportation, mining, and banking. Many Sukuma now live in cities with people from very different backgrounds and are exposed to many international influences.

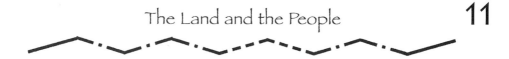

Tanzania has recently changed many of its socialist policies, which were introduced in the 1960s. In the past the socialist government controlled the economy and allowed no other political parties. Now Tanzania is rapidly moving toward democracy; it has increased its communication networks, and its economy is open to the world. This has brought many new job opportunities. It has also influenced the traditional culture of the Sukuma and all other Tanzanians.

▼ LANGUAGE ▼

In primary and secondary schools throughout the country, children are taught the Swahili language, Kiswahili. Tanzania is one of the few African countries that did not adopt the language of the European nation that colonized it. Kiswahili is spoken in Tanzania, Kenya, and in parts of Uganda, Zaire, Zambia, and many other countries. It is one of the diplomatic languages of the United Nations.

The Sukuma and all other Tanzanian cultures are united through the national language of Kiswahili. This makes it easier for people from different groups to communicate. Like the other ethnic groups of Tanzania, the Sukuma also have their own language, Kisukuma. It is the first language learned by most Sukuma children.

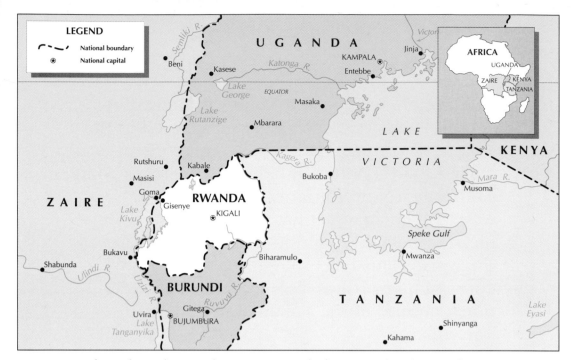

The Sukuma live mainly in Tanzania, which is considered part of east Africa, but they also have strong links with central Africa. The first Sukuma kings are said to have arrived in Usukuma from the west.

▼ USUKUMA ▼

The Usukuma region is only a few hundred miles south of the equator. Here the temperature remains between 60 and 100 degrees Fahrenheit year-round. There are short rains from September through October and longer rains from February to May. After the short rains, the temperature rises until the heat is broken by the start of the long rains in February. People depend on the rains to irrigate their fields and to provide water for their cattle.

The landscape of Usukuma is most notable for its rocky outcrops, called kopjes. These consist of enormous rocks balanced on top of each other. The land is very fertile in the north and near Lake Victoria, but dry to the south toward the city of Shinyanga. During a good rainy season a family can produce enough food for the entire year.

▼ WORK ▼

The Sukuma are cattle herders and farmers. Most people farm the land for rice, cassava, potatoes, and corn. In rural areas the cultivation of the farm, or *shamba* in Kiswahili, is a necessary part of daily life. Some Sukuma also grow cotton as a cash crop. Farming is a family activity. The family works together to grow enough food for the coming year.

In addition to their farmwork, both men and women in rural areas often seek wage-paying jobs in nearby towns. In larger villages and city centers, many women work as teachers, nurses, administrators, and businesswomen. They have little free time, since they also have family responsibilities after work.

Most women in rural areas work full-time tending to the needs of their families. A woman's daily routine begins with a search for firewood, then a walk to the well for the day's water supply. Next, she cooks a stiff porridge called *ugali*, which is an important part of the Sukuma diet. Women walk to the market often. There they both buy supplies and grind their

Rural life in Usukuma centers on herding cattle and farming (top). There are many rocky outcrops in the region, such as this burial place of Sukuma royalty (middle). Usukuma borders on Lake Victoria, where brightly painted boats are used by Sukuma fishermen (bottom).

corn at the mill. Children help their mothers with the day's chores, such as fetching water or sweeping the home and courtyard.

▼ ARCHITECTURE ▼

Throughout Usukuma the layouts of family homesteads have many common features. However, within the homesteads, there are several different styles of houses. In rural areas, a mixture of round houses, or *msonge*, and modern rectangular houses, or *ibanda*, can be found.

Historically, the Sukuma built round houses. They used wooden poles to form the basic structure and then filled the framework with wet clay.

There are three types of round *msonge* in use today: the *igumbule*, the *mhagale*, and the *maji*. The *igumbule* has one round room. Slightly more complex is the *mhagale*, which has an inner chamber, where parents and children sleep, and an encircling corridor, where the older children and the family's animals sleep. This is also where women cook the family's meals. A *maji*, the third style, is a smaller version of the *igumbule*, and is usually built by the grown sons of the homestead.

The roof of a *msonge* is thatched with straw, which keeps the house warm at night and cool during the day. Many people still build *msonge*, but rectangular houses are also now common.

Some say that rectangular houses became popular when logging began in the region. Fewer trees were available for *msonge* construction. *Ibanda* are built with sunbaked clay bricks set with a clay mortar. Most often there are two to three rooms within the house. Such a house can also have many rooms, depending on the wealth of its owner and the size of the family.

Traditionally, *ibanda* have thatched roofs, but tin roofs, called *bati*, are now gaining popularity. *Bati* are better than thatch for collecting the rainwater that runs off the roof during the rainy season. This collection of rain is necessary, since water is scarce in the dry season. However, tin roofs make it very hot inside the house. A tin roof is a sign of status because it is much more expensive than a thatched roof.▲

chapter

2

HISTORY AND POLITICS

TWO COMMON MISUNDERSTANDINGS EXIST
about Africa. The first is that African societies
do not have a long history. The second is that
these societies did not have political structures
before the Europeans colonized the continent.
Neither idea is true.

African civilizations prospered over many centuries. They created strong cultural traditions
and government structures that were maintained
from generation to generation and from leader
to leader. The traditional Sukuma customs of
today were formed in this way. They have
endured, while sometimes absorbing influences
from Africa, Arabia, Europe, and America.

During the Berlin Conference (1884–1885)
European governments divided Africa among
themselves. They created most of the international boundaries on the modern map of Africa.
These geographical divisions ignored the

traditional boundaries the African peoples themselves had established.

The chiefdoms in Usukuma began to form in
the 1500s. Early on, the Sukuma people traded
with several neighboring chiefdoms, including
the Baganda who live in modern-day Uganda. In
the 1800s the Sukuma began trading with Arabs
on the east African coast and on the island of
Zanzibar.

The first European contact with Usukuma
came in 1857, when John Hanning Speke traveled from England to Lake Victoria. He was followed in the 1870s by the explorer David
Livingstone and later by missionaries from the
English Anglican Church Missionary Society
and the French Catholic Missionaries of Africa.
But it was Carl Peters who opened the way for
the German East Africa Company to colonize
what was to become the country of Tanganyika,
later renamed Tanzania. He did this by signing
treaties with leaders and chiefs in order to
exploit them for economic gain.

The German colonists governed by military
force; they were oppressive and forced unfair
laws on the local people. Many rebellions challenged the German rule. After the Germans
were defeated in World War I in 1918, they were
forced to hand over Tanganyika to the British,
who had already colonized Uganda and Kenya
to the north.

In the early 1950s, under the leadership of Julius Nyerere, the Tanganyika Africa Association, a collection of farm cooperatives, joined other political organizations to become the Tanganyika African National Union (TANU). With the rallying call of *uhuru na umoja*, meaning freedom and unity, Tanganyika gained its independence in 1961. TANU's leader, Nyerere, became president of the country. Unlike other African independence movements, Tanganyika's transition to independence was peaceful and did not involve ethnic conflict.

In 1964 Zanzibar joined Tanganyika and the country was renamed Tanzania, a combination of the names of both territories. TANU developed into a new political party called Chama Cha Mapunduzi (CCM). Tanzania's most difficult task was preserving and respecting the many different cultures in Tanzania while encouraging them to work together to build their country.

In 1967 the famous Arusha Declaration was made. It put into practice President Nyerere's socialist policies and the Ujamaa Village Program. These strategies were intended to gather rural people together into organized communal villages to share technology, education, and medical services. However, to achieve this goal, the government forced people to move from areas where their families had lived for generations into unfamiliar new villages. Resistance to these moves, and the fact that local officials were sometimes corrupt, prevented Tanzania's Ujamaa policy from working.

Tanzania has experienced many hardships since independence. Today Julius Nyerere, known as Mwalimu, the Teacher, is fondly remembered for leading the nation to independence and for instilling patriotism among all Tanzanians. He united people through the language of Kiswahili and by creating a sense of responsibility to modernize their country.

Nyerere's policies aimed to improve the terrible conditions that his country experienced under colonialism. He also fought against problems in other African countries stemming from colonial rule. He assisted Uganda in removing its brutal dictator Idi Amin from power. He also strongly supported the African National Congress, which fought against apartheid rule in South Africa. His leadership is widely respected throughout Africa and around the world.

In the 1980s Ali Hassan Mwinyi was chosen to be the next president by President Nyerere and the CCM. In October 1995 Tanzania held its first multiparty election and the CCM candidate Benjamin William Mkapa was elected president. These presidents have slowly removed government control of industries, allowing the capitalist free-market system to grow.▲

CHIEFS AND ROYAL
TRADITIONS

ACCORDING TO **S**UKUMA ORAL HISTORY, THE
first *ntemi,* or chief, was Sanga. His power was
passed down to him from his uncle, Nkanda.
Nkanda was the son of Chief Muletwa, who
ruled in Lukalanga.

▼ THE FOUNDING OF THE ▼
SUKUMA CHIEFDOMS

One day Nkanda was sent east on a hunting
expedition by his father. While on his journey,
Nkanda stopped for water and said, "*Inye
Nsukumala aha,*" which means let us rest or stay
here. This could be the first reference to the
word *sukuma,* which is now the name of the
Sukuma cultural group. The village that Nkanda
founded is still called Sukumalaha. It is the first
of the fifty-two Sukuma chiefdoms.

Another version of early Sukuma history states
that the Waruli people, who lived in the area
where Nkanda decided to settle, believed that

Nkanda had strong powers. They thought that he could control rain, make people and animals fear him, and ward off crocodiles. The Waruli were so impressed by Nkanda that they invited him to become their chief. Nkanda declined the offer, citing the customs of his own people. It was required that a leader be descended not from a chief—as Nkanda was—but from a chief's daughter. Instead, Nkanda traveled back to his father's village, where his father chose the son of Nkanda's sister as the leader for the new region. This son, Sanga, became the first chief of the Usukuma.

Both stories make it clear that

All Sukuma chiefdoms have long histories dating back to the 1500s. Seen in this turn-of-the-century photograph is Mazangua, son of the Bukumbi chief, and his wife.

Nkanda was the key figure in forming the Sukuma people. Nearly every clan and chiefdom formed after Nkanda's time claims to be descended from this heroic founder of Usukuma.

Today the traditional greeting of the Sukuma chiefdom is *iminza*, a reference to Minza, Chief Sanga's mother. This greeting honors both the first chief and his family ties farther to the west. In reply to this greeting, a person gives the family name of one of his or her grandparents. The reply shows the continuing importance of loyalty to the chiefdom and family. It also helps to prevent marriages between people who are from the same clan and are, therefore, too closely related.

▼ THE ROLE OF THE *NTEMI* (CHIEF) ▼

In the 1500s the Sukuma first began to form chiefdoms rather than live in scattered villages. Since that time the role of the *ntemi*, or chief, has gone through many changes.

The word *ntemi* comes from the Kisukuma verb *kutema*, which means to cut down trees or to clear bush. This recalls the role of the early chiefs, who blessed the land when it was cleared at the beginning of each farming season.

The *ntemi* was responsible for keeping his chiefdom in the state of *mhola*, which means peace, health, and prosperity. If the chiefdom was at peace, the *ntemi*'s position was secure. If the chiefdom was unstable, the *ntemi* could be removed from office and replaced by another family member.

The *ntemi* traditionally served as a link between his subjects on the one hand and the royal ancestors and God on the other. The *ntemi* thus maintained the well-being of his people by serving as a priest or middleman of spiritual forces.

Today the *ntemi*'s religious and royal powers are still revealed to his subjects during ceremonies. These ceremonies include his enthronement and seasonal festivals connected with the annual farming cycle. In the past, ceremonies were also conducted before going into battle.

▼ THE ROYAL COURT ▼

Before the colonial era and independence, the *ntemi* was chosen from among the sons of the previous *ntemi*'s daughters. The choice was made by members of the royal family (*banang'oma*). They served as official attendants, similar to the cabinet members and ministers of today's governments.

The *banang'oma* rarely revealed who the new ruler would be before the current ruler died. A new *ntemi* therefore had no preparation for his job and turned to the *banang'oma* for training and guidance.

The *ntemi* was also heavily influenced by traditional doctors, including healers, diviners, and

The Sukuma Museum in Mwanza plays a key role in preserving and teaching Sukuma tradition. Seen here is the Royal Pavilion, built in the shape of a king's stool. It houses the items of royalty.

rainmakers (*bafumu*). In addition, he relied on the advice and skill of the blacksmiths (*balongo*). Blacksmiths had the important task of forging farming tools and weapons. They also controlled the use of fire in the community.

The royal court of the *ntemi* was linked both spiritually and economically with the blacksmiths and traditional doctors. These professionals aided the *ntemi* in royal and religious ceremonies, the creation of rain and fire, and the making of hoes and spearheads.

Any or all of these court authorities might be held responsible if the peace and prosperity of the chiefdom was challenged. They could be punished for mistakes, poor predictions, or bad

Colonial governments attempted to influence Sukuma chiefs during the colonial period. This turn-of-the-century photograph shows Masuka, a Sukuma chief of the Mwanza region.

advice upon which the *ntemi* may have acted. In this way the semidivine *ntemi* was shielded from daily criticism.

▼ THE *NTEMI* SINCE COLONIZATION ▼

The roles of the *ntemi* changed both during colonial rule and after independence.

During the periods of both German (1890–1918) and British (1918–1961) rule, the Sukuma chiefs were directly appointed by the colonial governments. The *ntemi* was no longer selected from the sons of the chief's daughter. Nor was he chosen by the *banang'oma*. Instead, the colonial governments appointed the chief. The Germans, for example, often placed leaders

from non-Sukuma coastal groups in power in Usukuma.

The British practiced a policy of indirect rule. They aimed to control the Sukuma by making the local chiefs enforce British colonial laws and policies. Under this approach, the *ntemi* became a civil servant of the colonial government. He was the main connection between it and the chiefdom. The authority of the *ntemi* was no longer traditional; instead it came from the British. During the more than seventy-five years of colonial rule, the role of the *ntemi* was greatly reduced. The Sukuma began to associate their own chiefs with the British and with a general lack of leadership.

It was not surprising that the political power of all chiefs was removed when Tanganyika became independent in 1961. On the eve of Independence Day, the future president Julius Nyerere said: "We tell the chiefs frankly that their authority is traditional only in the tribes; Tanganyika is not a traditional unit at all, and if the chiefs want to have a place in this thing we call Tanganyika, they have got to adapt themselves to this new situation; there is nothing traditional in the central government of Tanganyika."

▼ THE *NTEMI* TODAY ▼

After more than thirty-five years without royal authority, chiefs are now resurfacing in

Usukuma chiefdoms, including those of Magu, Nela, Busamabu, Ng'wagala, and Mwanza.

In 1992 Ntemi Kishina reinstalled himself as chief of the Bulima chiefdom with the help of his *banang'oma* (royal advisers). He used royal objects from his ancestors and others made by the *banang'oma* for the ceremony. Ntemi Kishina continues to make offerings for rain much like his ancestors did. He claimed great success for the good rains of 1994 and 1995.

As part of a revival of interest in *utamuduni*, or Sukuma traditions, chiefs are once again playing a role in Sukuma society. Seen here is Ntemi Kishina of the Bulima chiefdom. Around his neck and on his wrist are traditional royal ornaments made from shells.

Similarly, in the Ng'wagala chiefdom, Ntemi Kishosha Kapunda resumed the royal tradition of shaving his head to begin the planting season of 1994. In 1996 in the Nela chiefdom, Ntemi Masanja also shaved his head for the first time since independence, over thirty-five years ago.

As part of his reinstallation, Ntemi Masanja also had new royal drums made and decided to build a traditional royal house—one of very few in Usukuma. The royal house is large and has a special roof ornament at its peak. The ornament is based on two circles woven of thorn branches from the *makamila* tree. An inverted pot is placed above the thorns, together with four gazelle horns that point north, south, east, and west.

A traditional hoe, in the shape of a triangular spade, is placed on top of the arrangement and anointed with python fat, red ocher, rain medicine, and wild honey. Symbolically, the hoe represents the harvest, the earthen pot signifies plenty of food, and the thorn twigs suggest protection against the chiefdom's enemies. Ntemi Masanja's new royal house revives the customs of the past chiefs.

Today chiefs are trying to fulfill a role of cultural leadership. This is why they are renewing traditional customs and ceremonies, making new chiefly objects, and rebuilding their royal residences. Both chiefs and the government now

realize that there is an important role for chiefs to play as cultural—rather than political—leaders. As a result, chiefs have become much more visible and now take more active roles in their communities. This is one aspect of the increased interest in *utamuduni*, traditional culture, that is now spreading throughout Usukuma.▲

chapter

4

RELIGION

THE PEOPLE IN USUKUMA FOLLOW MANY
different religions today. Some practice traditional religion, while others are Muslim or Christian.

Before the arrival of Arab traders, Christian missionaries, and colonial governments, the Sukuma had an organized religion that was practiced within the family homestead.

Today those who still practice traditional religion pray in the family homestead for good rainfall and prosperity. Their prayers are directed to the Supreme Being and Creator, who is known by several Kisukuma names: Lyuba, Liwelelo, Lubangwe, and Seba. Many of these names are associated with the sun. This does not mean that the Sukuma worship the sun, but rather that the Creator has sunlike qualities, looking down over the earth and providing a life-giving force.

Followers of Sukuma traditional religion also honor the eternal spirits of deceased relatives, who watch over the living members of the family. When a person dies, many believe that their spirit continues to live on in another realm. The family remembers its ancestors through special prayers and offerings of millet beer and cow dung. Millet beer, or *lwanga*, is a mixture of millet seed and water. It is regarded as the favorite brew of the ancestors. The cattle dung, which is placed on the ancestors' shrines, symbolizes the family's wealth. This is determined by the number of cattle the family owns.

If the ancestors are not remembered and honored through offerings, it is believed that the family might have bad luck or even illness. For example, when a child is sick, the parents generally consult a traditional doctor who will determine if the illness is caused by angry or offended ancestors. If so, the family may have to make special offerings to appease that ancestor, or even rename the child after the dead relative.

Children who survive life-threatening illnesses are often renamed after ancestors. The child might also be required to wear a necklace of beads with a triangular, polished shell in the center, called a *lupingu*, in honor of his or her female ancestors. These beliefs illustrate the ongoing relationships between the past generations and their living relatives.

The ancestors play a crucial role in Sukuma religion. Here Nyambani Shilinde, a traditional doctor also known as Mungu wa Pili (Second God), holds a shell "telephone" and a stone that are both used to make contact with the ancestors. The attendant behind him holds the *buyege* healing drum.

▼ *NUMBA YA MASAMVA* ▼
(ANCESTRAL SHRINES)

A special structure called *numba ya masamva* (house of the ancestor) is built to honor a family's ancestors. An area is cleared in the family courtyard for the building of two small "houses." These houses are made of wood from the branches of three different trees: *nama, male,* and *nselya.*

Ancestral houses are not thought of as dwellings. Rather, they are regarded as shrines for the memory of deceased relatives, or ancestors. One is built for the ancestors on the father's side and another for those on the mother's side.

To build the shrines, the branches of the three trees are stripped of their bark, placed into the ground in a circle, pulled together, and tied at the top. Three flexible twigs and long strips of bark are then tied around the branches to create a cone-shaped, basketlike structure.

The top of the *numba ya masamva* is often decorated with *ng'ochangoka,* a special thorn branch signifying that the deceased person was the family leader. Sometimes a large snail shell or a broken pot is placed on the top of the structure.

Near the two ancestral shrines, three stones are set on top of each other. They form another small "dwelling" where offerings of cow dung and millet beer are made during special occa-

These special structures are shrines to honor family ancestors. The one on the left, in the courtyard of a traditional doctor named Mbula, has a pot on top. The one on the right is an example built on the grounds of the Sukuma Museum. The Royal Pavilion can be seen in the background.

sions or in times of need. Makula Bulungute, a Sukuma traditional doctor, says that members of his family leave offerings for their ancestors before going to special dance competitions. He suggests that "if the ancestors are happy, they will bring good luck."

▼ ISLAM ▼

Islam was introduced to the east African coast as early as the 1100s. However, the religion did not take hold inland until Arab merchants began to establish trading camps there. The first Arab traders traveled to Lake Tanganyika in the mid-1700s and slowly moved north into Usukuma toward Lake Victoria.

The largest Muslim communities can be found in the cities. In Mwanza there are several mosques where large congregations gather. In more remote villages, Sukuma Muslims pray in smaller mosques.

Muslim worshippers all over the world regard Friday as the holy day. They pray five times each day: at 6 AM, 1 PM, 4 PM, 6 PM, and 8 PM. In many places a call to prayer is broadcast from loudspeakers at the tops of the mosques and can be heard from far away. This call is sung and reminds people to come to the mosque to pray.

▼ CHRISTIANITY ▼

In the 1870s Christian missionaries traveled from Europe to Tanzania. Both Catholic and Protestant missionaries formed local missions in Usukuma. Church missions provided many services, such as health care and primary schools for children. This attracted Africans to the missions, where some converted to Christianity.

Unlike many of the early Protestant churches, the Roman Catholic Church did not forbid the use of alcohol and tobacco. It even permitted some traditional singing and dancing. However, both churches insisted that people give up their traditional religious beliefs and the special

objects associated with ancestor worship before they could convert.

In Usukuma today, local culture and songs are often used in Christian religious services, which occur on Sundays and sometimes daily. The Bujora Catholic Church is one example of a church that is devoted to a mixture of Catholic religion and traditional Sukuma language, song, and dance.

▼ THE BUJORA CHURCH ▼

The Bujora Church was founded in 1952 as a place where Sukuma traditions were used to teach the Catholic way of worshipping. The former Bishop of Mwanza, Josef Blomjous, selected the town of Kisesa for the experimental church. He sent a Canadian priest, Father David Clement, to learn about Sukuma culture and to teach Catholicism in a style that would engage the Sukuma community.

Father Clement, known as Fumbuka Klementi in Usukuma, formed a group of elders to conduct research on Sukuma traditions. They called themselves Bana Sesilia, meaning People of Cecilia, after the Catholic patron saint of music. They helped Father Clement to experience local culture. They also composed many original Sukuma melodies with religious lyrics taken from the Bible. They performed religious plays that taught large audiences about

Christianity. Bana Sesilia and Father Clement
together introduced Sukuma music and dance
into Catholic worship.

Bujora remains an important center for teaching Catholic worship through the local culture.
Church services at Bujora include Sukuma
music and dance. In addition, the Bujora
Church is the first in Usukuma to be designed
in the same style as a traditional Sukuma round
house.

The Bujora Church is painted white with red,
blue, and black triangles decorating both the
interior and exterior. The triangles represent the
traditional Sukuma farming hoe, which is associated with food and life. Now, the triangles have
also come to symbolize the Catholic Trinity of
the Father, Son, and Holy Ghost. The color
choice is also significant—black represents the
people of Africa; blue, Lake Victoria; and red,
fire and life.

Inside the church, symbols associated with
the Sukuma chiefs are now also used to symbolize the Christian God. The altar is built in the
shape of a royal throne. The tabernacle, a box
that holds Communion items, resembles a
chief's house with a shield and crossed spears on
the door.

Bujora has also used religious festivals to
spread its teachings. In several Catholic parishes,
priests celebrated the Feast of Corpus Christi, a

day set aside to honor the Holy Eucharist as the "body of Christ." Following Christian traditions, they hosted a parade and threw flowers at the Eucharist. Because this Christian feast coincided with the Sukuma harvest, the celebration took on new meaning for the Sukuma. Many Sukuma people were attracted to the new religion in this way.

Today the Feast of Corpus Christi is called Bulabo, which means flowers in Kisukuma. The ceremony occurs at the same time as the beginning of the Sukuma dance season, which takes place from June to August after the harvest of local crops.▲

chapter

5

MEDICINE AND HEALING PRACTICES

TRADITIONAL DOCTORS CONTINUE TO PLAY A major social and medical role within the Sukuma community. In Usukuma it is possible to seek medical treatment from a traditional doctor, a medical clinic, or a hospital.

Today not all Sukuma consult traditional doctors. However, many people have close relationships with their traditional healers. These healers treat ailments such as malaria, stomachaches, and psychological problems. They combine a knowledge of local plants and Sukuma ancestral beliefs with their experience in making medicines to provide herbal remedies, amulets, good-luck medicines, and long-term care. Traditional doctors practice both herbal healing and divination methods that have a long history in Usukuma.

Traditional Sukuma medicines and practices have been influenced by surrounding peoples.

For centuries Lake Victoria has been used to transport goods throughout the region. Through this link, the Usukuma have come in contact with all neighboring groups within the area. There is also an increasing presence of *majini*, a traditional practice of spirit possession, which stems from Muslim and Arab influences.

In the past, there were many different types of Sukuma healers—a *ngemi wa mbula* counseled people about rain; a *nfumu wa ngoko*, or chicken diviner, advised about the future; and a *manga* specialized in spirit possession. Some doctors read the entrails of a chicken to see the future, while others used gourd rattles. Each doctor had his own methods, but most believed that their healing power depended on the goodwill of their ancestors. Today Sukuma people can consult these specialists, or they can see a general practitioner who can prescribe modern medicines.

Traditional doctors inherit *shitongelejo*, or objects used to remember the ancestors, from their deceased relatives. These objects, such as a fly whisk, gourd rattle, or beaded headband, are used in healing. They are said to stimulate the aid of the ancestors in curing a patient. Bulungute Muleka, the current leader of the Bagalu Dance Society and a famous traditional doctor in Usukuma, explains that his ancestors give him advice concerning the condition and treatment of patients. Nyumbani Shilinde often

The items used by traditional doctors, such as beaded headbands, fly whisks, and gourds, are strongly associated with their ancestors. Here they are seen in use by a young doctor named Mbula (top) and the senior doctor Bulungute Muleka (bottom), who is one of the most famous traditional doctors in Usukuma.

makes offerings to his ancestors and seeks medical guidance from his deceased grandmother, who was also a healer and his teacher. Mbula, a young healer, also makes offerings and uses *shitongelejo* when contacting his ancestors for assistance. The way of life followed by these traditional doctors is a living tribute to their ancestors, on whom they depend for their livelihood.

Most Sukuma doctors encircle their homesteads with a dense, protective hedge of euphorbia shrubs. Inside the homestead there may be several different areas for healing: one section for divination, one for the grinding of herbs, and another for mixing and prescribing medicine.

Other areas within healers' homesteads are sectioned off for ancestral shrines. Honoring the family's ancestors is crucial to a traditional doctor's success in healing. In some areas a doctor will build special structures for consulting patients and that also serve to honor the ancestors. There are two separate types of buildings, each with a distinctive style. One is dedicated to the honor of the father's ancestors, and the other honors the mother's ancestors.

Other doctors consult patients in round houses called *maduku*, which are thatched from top to bottom. Only traditional doctors build *maduku*. These advertise a healer's compound to those who pass by.

Bulungute Muleka is both a famous doctor and the leader of the Bagalu Dance Society. In front of him is a large root called Nyahinga, which is used in healing. Directly behind him, to the left, is a staff covered with an animal skin, which holds some of the most powerful medicines in the Sukuma region.

Most traditional doctors have their practices in rural areas because in the cities, the costs of running a business can be very high. City dwellers will sometimes travel great distances into the countryside for consultations. Wealthy Sukuma businesspeople and others might visit their trusted traditional doctor for a divination session or for good-luck medicines, called *samba*.

Not all Sukuma consult *bafumu*, traditional healers. Modern medicine and technically equipped hospitals are also widely used in Usukuma. Even some Sukuma traditional healers recognize the benefits of modern medicine. Several have suggested that only a traditional

doctor can cure certain ailments, while other cases require modern medical technology. Others have traveled to modern hospitals to get medical attention for illnesses, such as appendicitis. Big cities like Dar es Salaam and Mwanza have up-to-date medical facilities and supplies. This is seldom the case in rural Tanzania, where a sick person may have to walk for a day to reach the closest clinic.

With the renewed interest in Sukuma traditional culture sweeping Usukuma, many people are now interested in combining aspects of modern medicine with traditional Sukuma healing. Mahyegu Lupande, a Sukuma from Kanyama village, is one such person. He manages the African Clinic at the Bujora Cultural Center, where he combines his training as a medical officer with an interest in his family's history as traditional doctors.

As a member of the Sukuma Research Committee and a historian of Sukuma culture, Lupande knows a great deal about Sukuma traditions. He uses his training in both types of medicine to determine the best cure for patients. Lupande is likely to prescribe herbal Sukuma remedies for certain ailments and Western medicine for others.

The architecture of the African Clinic makes a clear separation between these two types of healing. A concrete building houses technical

Some Sukuma doctors, such as Mahyegu Lupande (above), combine both Western and Sukuma medical traditions.

equipment and Western-style examination rooms. A large separated area has ancestral shrines (*numba ya masamva*) and two traditional, thatched houses associated with traditional healers.

In the African Clinic, Lupande brings together two aspects of contemporary African life: traditional belief systems on the one hand and technical developments on the other. His work at the African Clinic symbolizes the cultural changes that are taking place in Usukuma. Here, instead of rejecting their cultural traditions, the Sukuma are combining them with daily life in a changing world.

▼ MARIAM SWEYA ▼

Mariam Sweya has a successful practice as a traditional healer in Nyamhongolo village. She has a signpost on the major Mwanza-Musoma road that advertises her power as a healer and her skill in *majini*, a healing practice related to Islam.

The layout of Mariam Sweya's homestead was communicated to her in a dream by her ancestors. The homestead is circular but not enclosed. Although she lives in a traditional round Sukuma home, her homestead area also has two modern, rectangular houses, or *ibanda*, with tin roofs. In addition, Sweya created a small swamp area in which she grows papyrus to honor both her grandmother and the region where her family once lived.

Mariam Sweya uses two healing houses in her practice. The first is called the *numba ya njiba*. Built in the oldest Sukuma style, it is a round structure with reeds piled up to create the walls and roof. The other, an *igaga*, is also round, but has a higher roof supported by timbers. The interior walls of the *igaga* are painted with red ocher spots, which relate to Maasai medicines and Mariam Sweya's partial Maasai heritage. The walls also have white spots that signify the purifying power of python dung.

During her divination sessions in the *igaga*, Mariam Sweya sits on a stool. She uses many objects from her ancestors, such as a fly whisk

Seen here is Mariam Sweya, a traditional doctor, and the two healing houses she uses in her work: a reed structure (top) and a walled house (bottom). Her divination equipment and even the red dots painted on the wall (bottom) are all connected to her ancestors.

and a beaded headband. She also shakes a gourd rattle to communicate with her ancestors, who help diagnose problems and predict the patient's future.

Mariam Sweya performs another type of divination in the *numba ya njiba*. Here the patients must spit on a handful of millet seed and then place the seeds under their pillows the night before they return to visit her. Mariam Sweya says this allows her to see into her patients' dreams, helping her to better understand their needs.

On the return visit, she uses a basket to toss a mixture of the millet seeds and cowrie shells in the air. She reads their formation as they fall. As the final part of the divination, Sweya tells the patients their future and may prescribe herbal medicines for healing.▲

Sukuma dancers say that drumming is the backbone of the dance. The Kadumu drummers seen above somersault over their drums to excite the crowd. The dance below, called Bogobogobo, celebrates farming. The leader, Methodi Ng'wana Emanueli (right), blows a whistle and dances with a grain basket and a whisk.

chapter

6

DANCE

DANCING IS AN IMPORTANT PART OF SUKUMA life. The Sukuma are famous throughout Tanzania for their creative dancing styles. Dancers perform and compete in annual competitions, creating new costumes and using new and old dances just as their ancestors did over 100 years ago.

Many of the current Sukuma dances may have been started by groups of migrant farmworkers. To help pass the long day and to keep up their energy, the workers composed songs and lifted their hoes to the rhythm of singing and drumming. Members of the dance troupe helped to work on each other's farms and also worked as a group for money. Such farming groups still exist. However, Sukuma dancing is not limited to farmwork.

The competitive dance season begins in June, when people have free time from their farmwork

and can celebrate their new supply of food for
the year. The season can last through August or
until people resume their farming activities. A
good harvest is celebrated by an exciting season
of singing and dancing.

Dance festivals take place in a large field that
has been cleared for dancing, or in a small
stadium. A competition can be as short as a day
or as long as two weeks, depending on the occa-
sion or the number of participating dance
groups. Two of the biggest festival days for
dancers are national holidays that honor farming
and commerce in Tanzania: July 7, called Saba-
Saba, and August 8, called Nane-Nane.

Competitive dancing in Usukuma began with
the formation of two dance societies: the Bagika
and Bagalu. These societies were started in the
mid-1800s by two famous dancers and composers, Ngika and Gumha. Both of these men
lived for many years with traditional doctors to
gain the knowledge of magical medicines.

Because both were also famous dancers in
Usukuma, they were challenged to compete
against each other in dance to see who had the
most powerful medicines. Both used their magical potions to attract the spectators to their side
of the dance field and to force bad luck on their
opponents. The matches between these men
were fierce. In the end their supporters sided
with the performer they thought best. Ngika

then became the first leader of the Bagika Society, and Gumha headed the Bagalu. The Bagika and Bagalu societies are still going strong and continue to compete.

Today Bulungute, a grandson of Gumha, leads Bagalu. The leadership of Bagika is divided between Ibogo Muhangwa and Kabugume. These three men are considered to be very powerful because they have inherited their knowledge directly from the first dance society leaders, Ngika and Gumha. During the dance season Bulungute, Ibogo, and Kabugume are busy administering special medicines to their followers to help them win competitions.

Before going to a competition, the dance leader consults his trusted traditional doctor for special advice and good-luck medicines. He then wears certain medicines while the group is dancing or buries medicine in the dancing ground to bring good luck and to attract a crowd.

The most popular dance medicine is called *samba*. This is a special powdered form of good-luck medicine. It is believed to make the dancers, and especially the dance leader, very attractive to the audience. It can be used in three different ways. The dancers may mix the powdered medicine with lotion and rub it on their bodies; add some to their bathwater and allow it to wash over their bodies; or sit in an enclosed space,

Dance competitions are spiritual and magical events. Powerful medicines are used to bring luck and enhance performances during competitions. Seen here is a dramatic Bagalu dancer at the homestead of Bulungute Muleka.

hold the medicine over a fire, and allow the body's pores to "inhale" the substance.

During a competition some dancers build ancestral shrines on the dance ground. Larger structures are also built to house a constant fire to heat the *samba* medicine. At the competition, dancers go into the house to allow the smoking medicine to enter their bodies through the pores.

Performing at the same time, two dance groups try to win the crowd's favor at the dance competitions. Each attempts to perform the most outrageous stunts to draw the spectators over to their side. The crowd runs from one dance group to the other as the excitement builds and the cheers of the audience grow louder and louder. The winner is selected by judges based on the size of the crowd the dance group maintained during the competition.

Dance costumes are designed in many different styles. Dancers may create new costumes and dances each year in the hope of victory. One famous dance family, the Lyakus, create new moves every dance season. Hoja Lyaku, the family's grandfather, was a famous dancer of the Bakomyalume style. During a dance he would parade large wooden figures, often with movable arms and legs, in front of the spectators. The figures would draw a large crowd because of their novelty and humorous moves. Hoja's grandson, Steven Lyaku, decided that the family should stop using the wooden figures and find new ways to win. In 1995 Steven Lyaku won a dance competition when he wore a plastic monkey mask given to him by a Japanese traveler.

Maganigani is another young dancer who has achieved great fame in the Sukuma community through his innovative dances. He dances in the Sogota style, which he and his dance troupe

have helped to make popular all over Usukuma. Sogota dancers wear thigh-high, multicolored, striped socks. Their shorts and shirts are red with white designs. They also wear ankle bells that ring as the dancers jump high into the air and twist their bodies.

Maganigani consults his traditional doctor before the dance season. The doctor may give Maganigani and other Sogota dancers shallow cuts in their skin, into which medicines for attracting the dancing crowd are rubbed. To ensure good luck, the doctor prescribes special medicines and ways of honoring the ancestors. For example, Maganigani may build ancestral shrines on the dance ground and then perform in a special path around the structures.

Although he relies on traditional medicines for good luck, Maganigani's dance, Sogota, is very different from traditional Sukuma dances. Its originality has helped Maganigani become a popular star in Usukuma. Even in small villages children can be seen attempting to imitate the dance steps made famous by Maganigani. This blend of the traditional with the new is typical of the rich and dynamic culture in Usukuma today.

▼ WIGASHE: THE SITTING DANCE ▼

From June through September, Sukuma songwriters compete in long festivals. During the competition the composer, or *mlingi* in Kisukuma,

Costumes are a very important aspect of Sukuma dances. This performer wears a headdress made from heavy horns.

stands and sings. He is surrounded by his chorus group, called Wigashe (pronounced wee-gah-shay).

Wigashe competitions are also called sitting dances. This name arose because the chorus members sit on log benches around the leader and, as the song progresses, begin to jump from their benches in time with the song's rhythm. After the composer sings the words, the chorus echoes the song.

Composers write new melodies and complicated lyrics for every competition. Lyrics might cover anything from Sukuma history to recent elections, or may even carry a moral message about AIDS. In June of 1996 the composer Budelele's song commemorated those who died in a tragic ferry accident in Mwanza. Some composers write six or more songs each season.

Composers perform in intricate costumes of beaded, embroidered, or appliquéd vests, hats, and armbands. They sing and sway slowly while waving fly whisks. Most of the famous composers are men, but women also write songs and join in the chorus.

Like the dancers, composers are associated with either Bagika or Bagalu. Two composers compete at the same time (one from Bagika and one from Bagalu), use good-luck medicines, and try to attract a larger crowd than their opponents.

▼ DENMARK AND SUKUMA DANCING ▼

Denmark has a lively exchange with the
Sukuma culture. In the late 1960s several Danes
(people from Denmark) visited Bujora and other
areas of Usukuma. They formed a close relation-
ship with the Sukuma community, based on
their love of Sukuma dancing. Each year Danish
groups visit Usukuma to practice dancing and to
experience Sukuma culture.

Many Sukuma dance groups have been
formed in Denmark through these exchanges.
The Utamaduni (Culture) group was the first.
Some of the many other active dance groups in
Denmark are Watoto na Wengine (Children and
Others), Ikumbo (Whip), and Kisiwani (Of the
Island). These groups invite Sukuma dancers to
teach in Denmark each year. They also hold a
weeklong Sukuma cultural camp at the end of
July. Some Sukuma dancers have even settled
permanently in Denmark.

This exchange between the Danish and
Sukuma has been instructive to both peoples.
People in Denmark have the opportunity to
learn about African culture through Sukuma
dance classes and exhibitions. Likewise, the
Sukuma have learned about Danish culture.

The Danish have had an impact on Sukuma
dance. Some Danes have become famous for
their dancing in Usukuma and have even invent-
ed new moves for Sukuma dances. For example,

Many people come from Denmark to learn about Sukuma culture. The Danish often learn Sukuma dances and drumming during their stays and have even formed dance groups in Denmark devoted to Sukuma dancing. Here a Danish man, whose Kisukuma name is Madadi, which means "stilts," performs with a Sukuma dance group during a competition in Kisesa village.

one Danish man, whose Kisukuma name is Lubala, held dance classes for Sukuma children to practice Banungule, the porcupine dance, which he had learned through dance classes in both Denmark and Tanzania. In 1995 he taught the children a mixture of traditional Banungule steps, hip-hop, and break dancing. These additions gave a new flavor to a favorite Sukuma dance. They may soon become an important part of Banungule traditions.▲

Glossary

appliqué A cutout decoration that is attached to another, larger piece of material.

bafumu (**singular:** *nfumu*) Traditional doctors.

banang'oma A chief's advisers.

chiefdom A group of people and area of land organized under a chief.

cooperatives Organizations owned and operated by the same group of people.

divination The practice of using supernatural powers to see the future or discover hidden knowledge.

fly whisk A type of swatter made from an animal tail; often a symbol of great spiritual power in Africa.

iduku (**plural:** *maduku*) Traditional doctor's house.

masamva Ancestral spirits.

ntemi Chief.

socialism A political system in which the state owns and controls the means of production (factories, technologies, etc.).

tabernacle An ornamental box in which the elements of the Eucharist, or Communion, are kept.

utamuduni Traditional culture.

For Further Reading

Attwater, Donald. *The White Fathers in Africa.* London: Burns, Oates and Washbourne Ltd., 1937.

Cory, Hans. *The Ntemi: Traditional Rites of a Sukuma Chief.* London and Nairobi: East African Literature Bureau, 1951.

Liebenow, J. G. "The Sukuma, a Tanganyika Federation." In *East African Chiefs*, Audrey I. Richards, ed. London: Faber and Faber, Ltd., 1960.

Malcolm, D. W. *Sukumaland: An African People and Their Country.* London: Oxford University Press, 1953.

Stanley, Henry M. *How I Found Livingstone: Travels, Adventures and Discoveries in Central Africa.* New York: Charles Scribner's Sons, 1902.

Challenging Reading

Knudsen, B. R. "Dance Societies: The Voluntary Work-Associations of the Sukuma." *Tanganyika Notes and Records*, No. 81-82, 1977, pp. 66-74.

INDEX

AUTHORS' ACKNOWLEDGEMENTS

We would like to thank the Tanzanian Commission for Science and Technology, the village of Bujora, and the Sukuma Museum for their continuing encouragement of our research. We are indebted to the wisdom of the Sukuma community who has shared culture with us. We also wish to express our gratitude to Harvard University and the Fulbright Fellowship Committee for their support of our work on Sukuma culture and to Professor Suzanne Blier of Harvard University for being amazing.

ABOUT THE AUTHORS

Aimée Bessire is currently writing her dissertation on Sukuma arts and culture for Harvard University. She received an M.A. in Ancient Near Eastern and Twentieth Century Art from New York University's Institute of Fine Arts. She was also a Helena Rubinstein Fellow at the Whitney Museum of American Art.

Mark Bessire has spent the last year conducting research at the Sukuma Museum in Tanzania as a Fulbright Fellow in Museum Studies. He received an M.B.A from Columbia University and an M.A. in Art History from Hunter College of the City University of New York. He, too, was a Helena Rubinstein Fellow at the Whitney Museum, where he met his wife, Aimée.

PHOTO CREDITS

All photographs taken by the authors, except for historical photographs, which are courtesy of the Missionaries of Africa Archives, Rome.

CONSULTING EDITOR

Gary N. van Wyk, Ph.D.

LAYOUT AND DESIGN

Kim Sonsky